THE PASTOR'S SECRET
The D.L. Series

Kimberly Moses

Copyright © 2020 by Kimberly Moses

All rights reserved. No part of this publication may be reproduced, distributed or transmitted in any form or by any means, including photocopying, recording, or other electronic or mechanical methods, without the prior written permission of the publisher, except in the case of brief quotations embodied in critical reviews and certain other noncommercial uses permitted by copyright law. For permission requests, write to the publisher, addressed "Attention: Permissions Coordinator," at the address below.

Kimberly Moses/Rejoice Essential Publishing
PO BOX 512
Effingham, SC 29541
www.republishing.org

The Pastor's Secret/Kimberly Moses
ISBN-13: 978-1-952312-23-6

CONTENTS

PREFACE:..vii

CHAPTER ONE: The Last Confession............1

CHAPTER TWO: I Had Everything Until.....10

CHAPTER THREE: The First Encounter...........28

CHAPTER FOUR: I Got To Stop.....................41

CHAPTER FIVE: The Rampage.....................55

CHAPTER SIX: Revenge..............................63

CHAPTER SEVEN: Something Isn't Right.......78

CHAPTER EIGHT: Exposure............................92

CHAPTER NINE: I Lost Everything.............106

CHAPTER TEN: Death Is Waiting...............116

ABOUT THE AUTHOR...125

PREFACE

One day, I was watching a documentary about Black film history. There was a young gay man who wrote a film about two black men being passionately in love. The film won an award and righteous indignation filled my heart because that lifestyle is an abomination to the Lord (Leviticus 18:22). At that moment, I declared that I would write God a film to warn others about the risks of a homosexual lifestyle. I know first hand because I was involved in a relationship with another woman years ago until the Lord set me free. That relationship was chaotic and caused me to lose everything. I had anxiety for five years as a result.

To make matters worse, I tried to hide my sinful ways, and sadly many people in the church are actively involved in the same lifestyle but on the down-low or behind closed doors. They are pretending to live holy lives, but they aren't. The goal of this novel isn't to shame or condemn anyone but to bring the light of the gospel of Jesus Christ and to show the devastation of sin. The Lord gave me a series to expose the hidden works of darkness and bring about repentance.

Kimberly Moses
Founder of Rejoice Essential Magazine

CHAPTER ONE

THE LAST CONFESSION

It's a Tuesday afternoon at St. George's Triangle Hospital. The intensity of the atmosphere hung heavily as the medical staff paced through the halls. Shawn Wayne stared into the hallway as he laid in bed. He could hear alarms going off and the staff discussing his case. Dr. Frank Shirapo had given him a bad prognosis two days ago.

Dr. Frank Shirapo: Mr. Wayne. Your results show that you have (PCP) Pneumocystis carinii pneumonia and non-Hodgkin lymphoma. You are also septic. The mortality rate is high. Most people don't last very long. We will do all we can to save your life and make you comfortable. Do you have any questions? Do you have anyone you can call?

Shawn: "No. I'm all alone," as dread started to sink in.

Dr. Frank Shirapo: Very well. We will get someone from our medical staff to come to sit with you.

Shawn: Thank you, Doctor.

Dr. Frank Shirapo walks out of the room.

His nurse Susan had positioned his bed into the upright position a half an hour ago. St. George's Triangle Hospital was considered the top facility in neurology, but here Shawn laid dying.

Shawn: "I'm too young to die," he thought to himself. "It's been two weeks and I'm getting worse."

Shawn knew that his time was running out. His mind was full of fear, regrets, and disbelief. The fear of death overwhelmed him. He looked down at his wrist band as a reminder that this wasn't a dream but reality. He was shocked at how skinny his arms had become. His usual weight is 220 pounds, which is perfect for his 6'1 height. Now he is frail, only weighing 160 pounds.

Shawn could barely eat his meatloaf, broccoli, mash potatoes, and gravy served for lunch. After taking three bites of the meatloaf, he was done. He was able to wash it down with a couple of swallows of unsweetened ice tea.

Shawn: As good as this food looks, I'm just not hungry.

Susan: Mr. Wayne. You have to eat to gain strength. If you don't, then we will have to put in a feeding tube.

Shawn: "I will try," he said, disappointedly.

Susan was a young Asian nurse who had a bubbly personality. Her smile brightened up everyone's day. She would often hum the latest hit songs as she worked. She seemed to really care about her patients. The first day Shawn saw her, he knew she was trustworthy. He felt calm around Susan because she wasn't rude like some of the other nurses that he had encountered previously.

A few nights ago, he swore that a nurse named Josh tried to kill him. He was inexperienced and seemed lazy. Shawn kept complaining about abdominal pain and needed restroom assistance, but the nurse was nowhere in sight. He ended up having a bowel movement on himself. That was strike number one. His anger raged through him as he had to wait to be cleaned up fifteen minutes later. The stench of his feces filled the air. When Josh came into the room, Shawn gave him a piece of his mind.

Shawn: Man, I wish you would just do your job! I have been ringing this call bell for a while. No one should be treated like this!

Josh: Mr. Wayne, I apologize. There was an emergency down the hall. I got here as fast as I could.

Strike two was when Josh had a medicine mixup. He almost gave Shawn another patient's medication. Shawn didn't feel right about it.

Shawn: "You are trying to kill me! I don't trust you. I want another nurse," he snarled.

Josh: Mr. Wayne. I assure you that I'm doing my job, which is to provide you with excellent care.

Shawn: Then, why are you trying to give me Mrs. Johnson's medications? This bottle says her name.

Embarrassed, Josh takes the bottle from Shawn and apologizes. He then handed him the right medication.

Shawn: I would like to talk to your supervisor.

The head nurse, Florence, entered the room. She was an elderly woman with lots of experience.

Florence: Mr. Wayne. I apologize for any mistakes or inconvenience. We are assigning you a new nurse. Her name is Susan and you will love her.

Shawn: Sighed a breath of relief and laid his head back on the pillow.

As Susan moved the lunch tray that had been sitting for a couple of hours out of the way, Shawn's eyes followed the long nasal cannula connected to the wall pumping 6L of oxygen into his lungs. The tubing rested in his nostrils, behind his ears, and underneath his chin. Over the last weeks, his breathing has become labored. It seemed that he couldn't get enough air when he would walk. When he was admitted to the hospital, his oxygen saturations were 83% on room air. The 6L of oxygen increased his saturations to 98%.

Shawn's eyes began to look at the IV that was stuck in the back of his hand. Susan had just put a syringe of medicine in it. He could feel the cool medication coursing through his veins and knew relief was coming soon.

Susan: Mr. Wayne. You seem restless. Would you like to talk to the Chaplain? It might do you some good.

Shawn: Yes. I would love that.

Susan: Great. I'll make the call downstairs to the Chapel.

Shawn: Thank you.

Susan: "You're welcome," she said as she walked out of the room.

As Shawn waited for the chaplain to come, he started to feel weak again. His strength was leaving him each day. He didn't want to waste anymore energy by chasing cords, wires, and tubes with his eyes out of boredom. So he decided to rest. He needed to tell someone, who wouldn't judge his secret. He had been carrying this heavy burden and hated himself for all the evil that he had done ten months prior. The guilt, pain, and shame felt worse than a death sentence.

As Shawn started to doze off, there was a light tap on the door. He opened his eyes to see that the chaplain had finally arrived. Shawn was always a man of faith, so it felt reassuring to know he could speak to someone similar.

The chaplain was a middle aged, Caucasian man. His grey streaked beard told the story of wisdom even despite his young face. His older salt and pepper hair covering his head betrayed his youthful face. The chaplain walked up to Shawn's bed and extended his hand in greeting.

Chaplain Sam: Hi. I'm Sam. Nice to meet you.

Shawn: My name is Shawn.

The two men shook hands. Chaplain Sam pulled up a chair next to the bed.

Chaplain Sam: Susan tells me that you are restless and you need to talk to someone. I can remember when I was anxious during a dark time in my life. I was struggling to pay my way through college and didn't know how I was going to make it but the Lord came through for me. Another time, I felt scared was when my daughter was in a car accident and everyone thought that she wasn't going to make it. I had to use my faith and stand on the Word of God. Miraculously, she pulled through and now she is away at college.

Shawn: Amen. That is very encouraging. Your situation is different from mine. I'm a bad person. I did a lot of wicked things. The guilt I feel is eating me up inside.

Chaplain Sam: Mr. Wayne, I can relate. I know how that feels to be full of condemnation, but there is hope in Jesus Christ. Do you know Him?

Shawn: Yes. I knew him. I used to be a pastor of a mega church but sinned against Him. You probably heard of me. You are right about being full of condemnation. That's certainly my problem.

Chaplain Sam: Shawn, the Bible says, "As far as the east is from the west, so are your transgressions far from me. These aren't my words but God's. You may have messed up, but God is merciful. He loves you so much. Once you repent of those sins, He throws them into the sea of forgetfulness. The devil is the culprit behind the condemnation that you are feeling. Romans 8 verse 1 tells us that there is no condemnation of those who belong to Christ Jesus who walk in the Spirit.

Shawn: Yes. That's so reassuring to hear that. I have been allowing the devil to torment me. Every day, I live with the pain and agony of what I have done.

Tears began to stream down Shawn's face. Chaplain Sam handed him a Kleenex.

Shawn: "I've made a mistake and hurt so many people," he sobbed. "I don't even feel like God hears my prayers anymore and I feel so distant from Him."

Chaplain Sam: Sin does make us feel distant from God, guilty and condemned but there is hope. God is a God of multiple chances. Will you let him in your heart today?

Shawn: "Yes, but I need to confess my sins. I haven't talked about this since this happened. Now the doctors are saying that I don't have too much longer to live. I don't want to die carrying this baggage. I want to feel the peace of God again. So I know that when I die, I'll be in eternity with Him."

Chaplain Sam: You can tell me, Shawn. The Bible says to confess your sins to one another so you can be healed. I believe that as you clear your consciousness today, you will receive healing in your soul.

Shawn: It all started to go south when I met Donald.

CHAPTER TWO

I HAD EVERYTHING UNTIL....

My life was perfect. Many people considered our family a success story. I grew up poor, went to Bible college, got a doctorate degree, got married, and lived in a huge house. I went from rags to riches and never had to beg for anything. I grew up in a small town called Wagram, which was underdeveloped. We only had one gas station, a grocery store, a police station, and a schoolhouse. People laughed when I told them that it took about 4 to 5 minutes to drive through Wagram before entering the next town.

I had an older brother, but we were almost eleven years apart and never close. He left home early and joined the military. He rarely visited over the years, so I spent most of my childhood alone, wishing that I had more friends. My father was an alcoholic and would cheat on my mother. I remember him being away for several days at a time while my mother tried to mask her pain. She would hug me and tell me that everything was going to be okay. I remember one day, I was around five years old, and the phone kept ringing. My mother could no longer pretend that everything was alright.

Momma: Hello.

Misty: Where is Joseph?

Momma: I know you ain't calling here asking for my husband. Have you lost your mind?

Misty: Look! If you would've done your job, then he wouldn't be coming to me to get satisfied!

Momma: Shut the H…..!

Momma was about to curse because she was furious, but she stopped when I walked into the kitchen. It was as if I was the angel that stopped her from sinning. Momma slammed down the phone and twenty seconds later, it rang again.

Shawn: What's going on Momma?

Momma: Shawn. Let's go outside and sit on the porch.

Tears filled my mother's eyes as she took me by my hand and led me outside on the porch. It was a peaceful day. The sun was shining and there was a cool breeze present. The calmness of the outside drowned out the chaos of the phone ringing inside.

Shawn: What's wrong?

Momma: Baby. I am sorry that you have to see this. (She began to weep) Your daddy has a girlfriend and she keeps harassing me.

Shawn: It's okay. Momma, don't cry. Where is daddy?

In that moment, Shawn started to feel sad, angry, and confused. That was the day that hatred entered his heart for his father. He knew, even then, only momma should be daddy's girlfriend. He hated to see his mother who was a beautiful strong woman break down. He liked seeing his mother happy because she had the whitest most beautiful smile that he had ever seen. He admired his mother and he thought to himself, "One day, I'm going to marry a girl like momma."

Momma: I don't know, but let me worry about that. Let me tell you a story.

She wiped her tears on the back of her hands. She embraced Shawn, wrapping her arm around him and planting a kiss on his forehead.

Shawn was too young to understand all the details, but he knew that his mother didn't deserve to be hurt. Momma was a woman of faith and would read the Bible daily to gain strength. She would tell him Bible stories, which inspired him, years later, to become a pastor.

Momma: Once upon a time, there was a man named Moses. He had a brother named Aaron and a sister named Miriam. God chose them to do a great work on the earth. There was a mean old King, named Pharaoh, who enslaved all God's people. One day Moses was walking in the wilderness and he saw a bush burning. Out of the bush, he heard the voice of God. The Lord told him that he was going to be a deliverer and that he would go to Egypt to do a great work. Moses didn't think he could do the job because he had a stuttering problem. So, God reconnected him with his brother and sister, who were both prophets so they could assist him.

Momma began to tell the story of the Israelites in Egypt, Moses, and the Red Sea. It was actually one of Shawn's favorites because he visualized himself doing a great work for God one day as well. They sat outside for a while until it was time to get ready for bed.

One day, there was barely any food in the house. Daddy was back and he sat on his recliner all day drinking his liquor and mocking my mother's faith. I knew it bothered her, but she stayed strong and rarely argued with him.

Daddy: You are nothing but a holy roller. Pray to your God to get some food in this house!

Momma: God will supply all our needs according to His riches and glory in Christ Jesus!

Daddy: Blah, blah, blah. Your God ain't nothing!

Momma: Be careful about mocking the Lord. I pray that you repent before He strikes you down.

Daddy: You repent for being stupid. You ain't nothing. I made you.

Momma knew that it was pointless arguing with a drunkard. She recognized that she was arguing with a demonic spirit, so she surrendered her control and thought, "Lord, deal with him because I can't. This man is driving me insane."

She had recently got a job in the next town over as a janitor cleaning up motel rooms. My father always spent the bill money on alcohol and his fast lifestyle so she had to work to make sure we were taken care of.

Momma: I am going to work, guys. See you in a few hours.

Shawn: Bye, momma.

Shawn grew sad when she left because his father would ignore him. He acted as if he hated Shawn and rarely showed any affection. Shawn knew that his father didn't want him around, so he went to his room and started playing with GI Joes. Fifteen minutes after his mother was gone, his father picked up the phone and called his mistress.

Daddy: Hey baby. What are you doing?

Misty: Nothing. Thinking about you.

Daddy: Come show me how much you miss me. The house is ours for a few hours.

Misty: Umm. I have Junior with me.

Daddy: Bring him. He can play with Shawn.

Misty: Okay. We will be there in a few minutes.

Daddy hung up the phone and about ten minutes later, Misty and her son, Junior, came over.

Misty: Junior go into the back room and play with Shawn.

Junior obeyed. He was around eleven years old and heavy set. As Junior left the room, Misty and Daddy started to kiss passionately while groping each other in their private places. They held hands and went into the bedroom. At first they tried to be quiet, but moaning eventually erupted in the heat of the moment. They had sex for about 45 minutes. While they were away, another turn of events was about to take place in Shawn's room.

Junior: I don't want to play GI Joes anymore.

Shawn: Well, I have video games.

Junior: I don't want to play video games.

Immediately, Junior pushed Shawn down to the ground while pulling off his pants and underwear. They wrestled back and forth as Shawn tried to pull them back up. Shawn's face was buried in the carpet.

Shawn: Get off of me. Daddy! Help!

Junior: Shut up fool! They can't hear you!

Daddy couldn't hear Shawn's cries for help because he was screwing Misty in the other room. Through Shawn's cries, Junior rears back and punched him in the mouth and threatens him. He weighed twice as Shawn. Shawn's buttock is now exposed and Junior rapes him. It was very painful as he was penetrated. It lasted for about five minutes and it was a horrific experience that altered Shawn's destiny. Shawn was terrified and laid frozen in his room until his mother came home from work several hours later. Twenty minutes after the rape, Junior and Misty left the house. Daddy never came to check on Shawn because he passed out on his recliner drunk.

It was after midnight when momma arrived home. She saw her husband passed out in the living room. She didn't bother him. When she went into her son's room to check on him, she knew something was wrong. Shawn was still lying on the floor in the same spot. His pants were down and his butt was still exposed. She could tell that he had been crying because of the dried stains on his face. She scooped him up in her arms and cried. She knew that her son was hurt. She started to pray. Shawn woke up but he was still shocked by the previous events and laid stiff. Tears fell from his eyes.

Momma: Lord, show me what happened. My baby is hurt and I pray it's not what I think it is.

Before momma could finish the prayer, she went into a vision. She saw the events play out before her eyes. She saw Misty and Junior arrive twenty minutes after she had gone to work. She saw Misty and her husband sleeping around in her bedroom. Then she saw her son get beat up and raped.

Momma: Oh no! Lord, say it ain't so! Lord, enough is enough. How could this happen? I serve you. I go to work to take care of my family and my son isn't safe when I am gone. Make my husband pay, God. I can't take it anymore! If you don't do something God then I will kill him! Do it God!

Momma held her son and cleaned him up. She rocked him to sleep. She promised to never allow anything to happen to him again. She ended up quitting her job because she was afraid that something would happen to her son. The next day, Momma confronted Daddy about the incident but he denied the whole thing. A couple of days went by and the atmosphere was still tense.

Daddy: I'm going to the store to get some beer.

Momma: Okay.

Daddy left the house and as he drives through the stoplight, a car comes out of nowhere and slammed directly into him. When the vehicle T-boned him, Daddy was killed instantly. The driver was intoxicated and wasn't paying attention when they rammed into him, smashing the car, and crushing Daddy. The paramedics arrived at the crash scene several minutes later. Since Wagram is such a small town, everyone knew everybody. People began to talk and someone called Momma with the tragic news. Momma didn't want to believe it but when the Sheriff came to the door an hour later, she knew it was a reality. Momma was shocked. She closed the door and slid down the wall. At that moment, her prayer came back to her remembrance.

Prayer: Make my husband pay, God. I can't take it anymore! If you don't do something God then I will kill him! Do it God!

Momma always carried guilt that she was the cause of her husband's death. Twenty years later, as she laid in her hospital bed dying from breast cancer, she confessed the guilt that she had carried for so long. A few days later, Momma was dead.

I struggled with my sexuality throughout the years but always dismissed it. I couldn't allow my mind to go there because it's an abominable act in the sight of God. I never told anyone what happened and the battle I faced. I believe in the deliverance power of the Lord. I went to Bible College because I loved the Lord. The stories that my mother told me as a kid were imprinted in my memory. I obtained a doctorate in Theology.

Life was good. I was out of Wagram and living in Charlotte. I enjoyed the city life. God was opening doors and my preaching ministry had officially begun. A pastor saw a video clip of my preaching on social media and he invited me to be the main speaker for their annual revival in Columbia. I was excited because I had no idea that I was about to meet the woman of my dreams.

During the Friday night service, I first laid eyes upon the lovely Connie. Her name is Casandra but everyone calls her Connie. Her skin was radiant, an almond hue and she had a glow. It was as if the Lord was highlighting her to me. At that moment, I knew she was the one. She had the prettiest whitest smile like my mother. Her hair was long and framed her face beautifully. She was fine and had a nice shape. I couldn't get distracted by her beauty because I was on assignment. After the service, I met people and shook their hands. Then Connie approached me. Let me put on a straight face, so she won't know that I am interested.

Connie: That word blessed me. It was confirmation.

Shawn: Praise Him, sister.

Connie: I have been waiting for my breakthrough but after tonight…..(She gets cut off because several people are waiting to talk to Shawn).

Pastor: Excuse me, Dr. Wayne. They are waiting for you in the back.

Shawn: Thank you. I am coming. (The pastor stands to the side as he waits for Shawn to finish his conversation).

Shawn then pulls out a business card and hands it to Connie.

Shawn: You can further connect with my ministry by calling my office phone. Call me, okay?

Connie: Okay.

Shawn walked away toward the back offices. What Shawn didn't know is that Connie thought he was attractive as well. During the following week, Shawn was in his office and his phone rings.

Shawn: Hello.

Connie: Can I speak to Dr. Shawn?

Shawn: This is he.

Connie: Hello. I don't know if you remember me, but my name is Cassandra. Everyone calls me Connie. I met you in Columbia at a revival service. I was trying to tell you how I got a breakthrough but the pastor interrupted. You gave me your card and told me to call.

At that moment, Shawn knew it was the woman he had noticed during the service. How can he forget? He knew that she was his wife.

Shawn: Of course, I remember. That was a powerful service. I'm so blessed to know that you got what you came for.

Connie: Yes. When you were preaching, I felt the presence of God so strong and I received a breakthrough. I was praying to feel His presence again and He used you to bless us.

Shawn and Connie continued the conversation for the next few minutes. They laughed but Shawn had a meeting and would have to cut it short.

Shawn: Excuse me if I am out of order but can I take you to dinner?

Connie: You aren't out of order. I would love to go.

Shawn: Ok great. Text me your address and I will pick you up Friday night.

Connie: Ok. Have a good day.

Shawn: You too.

They hung up the phone and both were excited about their new friendship. From that moment, they were inseparable. They talked everyday and text throughout the day. When they saw each other's messages, their faces would light up. When Friday night came, they went out to an Italian restaurant. They both were dressed to impress. They laughed and talked. They had a good time. When they weren't in each other's presence, they missed each other. Six months later, they married. They spent their honeymoon on a five-day cruise to the Caribbean. They made love every day for hours and the only time they left their cabin was to get something to eat on the dock. They enjoyed pleasuring one another. They were the answer to each other's prayers.

Shawn had never been with a woman and he struggled with his attraction to men. He never told his wife about the rape. He figured that she would view him differently if she knew. Connie just fit in. She was his rib and a true helpmeet. She made Shawn better and helped him stay organized. Shawn pushed Connie and helped her walk-in her destiny. They both were active in the community. They were feeding the homeless, ministering at the prison, and doing videos on social media. They grew successful as they launched their church. They had many sons and daughters in the faith. It was amazing how eleven years after they first opened, they grew to be a megachurch. Connie and Shawn were happy. They had annual conferences that were known all over the globe. People from all nations would travel to attend. Their house had curb appeal and was one of the biggest homes in the neighborhood. They were planning a family vacation to go to a ski resort. They had many plans but they didn't realize that the devil was watching and waiting for an opportune moment to strike.

Shawn kept a photo of his mother on his desk. He missed her and wished that she was alive so she could see his life now, meet his wife and daughter. Tonight was the big meeting, Shawn was the opening speaker. He was preparing for service. While walking through the lobby at the church, a few men walked through the doors. One of the men was Donald but everyone called him Donnie. The two locked eyes and Shawn started to get aroused but he looked away. He didn't know what happened. "What am I doing? I can't be attracted to this man. He is nice looking but I have Cassandra and she satisfies me sexually. I can't sin against God. So why did I just get aroused when I looked into this man's eyes. Lord help. Those feelings are arising again."

Deacon Brown: Excuse me Pastor. I want to introduce you to Donnie. He is new here and looking to join.

Shawn: Praise him young man. Nice to meet you. We are having our annual conference tonight. I pray you will join us.

Donald: Yes. I am excited. I will be around. I came here to serve.

Shawn: Great. If you are with Deacon Brown, then you are in good hands. He will take care of you. See you guys tonight.

Shawn walks away saying bye to the crowd of men. He went into his office and shut the door. He had a slight erection. His mind flashed back to Donald. He felt an attraction there. He wrestled in his mind for several minutes and began to rebuke those wicked thoughts.

Shawn: In the name of Jesus. I command you O foul devil to leave out my mind.

Immediately as those thoughts came, they left and Shawn exhaled. Knock. Knock. Knock. The sounds of knocking interrupted his thoughts.

Shawn: Come in.

Connie: Hey baby.

Shawn: Hey. You came at the right time. I am ready for you. I'm thinking about taking you right here.

Connie: Umm. Is that right? I'm ready for you too.

Shawn is still erect. Connie walks in and shuts the doors. She locks it. She starts to undress and the two make love.

CHAPTER THREE

THE FIRST ENCOUNTER

The conference was so powerful. The altar was full of people crying out to God and people kept talking about how it blessed their lives for several days afterward.

Several weeks after the conference, Shawn's schedule began to slow down. He only had to focus on preparing for the Wednesday night word and the Sunday message. He and Connie weren't booked to travel anywhere. The deacons at the church took the burden of the outreach ministry where the homeless were fed biweekly off his shoulders. Shawn knew that this was the opportune time to write some sermons for the weeks to come and rest. Connie was at the house starting up a new business venture. She was so creative and very hard working. Her great grandmother passed down a formula to make a variety of scented candles.

Connie had the pots, ingredients, wicks, jars, and labels to launch her products. She launched her website and had the church's support. She had so many orders and the demand kept her busy. As she worked the kitchen and the utility room would be cluttered. She was in her own zone and Shawn knew that she didn't want to be bothered.

Shawn: Baby, I'm going to my office at the church to study. I'll see you later.

Connie: Ok, baby.

Connie walked over to Shawn as he stood at the front door ready to leave and pecking his lips. She was a foot shorter than her husband and had to stand on her tippy toes to kiss him. Shawn grabbed his wife's bottom.

Shawn: I will get some of that later.

Connie: Hmm. Don't keep me waiting too long.

Shawn walked out the door and drives to the church. During his drive, thoughts of perversion started to come into his mind out of nowhere. Then Donald's attractiveness came into his mind. He was built well so much so that his muscles could be seen underneath his shirt. His skin was almond colored and he was tall. Shawn didn't realize that he was making a mistake by not rebuking those thoughts. At first he was able to resist the enemy but eventually he grew weary and gave in to those thoughts. He knew he needed to talk to someone about how he was feeling but was too ashamed. He knew that he was bound and needed deliverance. Yet, he was so scarred from his childhood rape and too embarrassed to even mention it to his wife. There was a cloud of confusion over his mind and sometimes he even doubted his identity in Christ.

"What will people think about me if they found out that I was attracted to another man? I am a pastor but my mind is very wicked. I'm not even feeling the presence of God as I used too. I feel so far from Him. I can't pray or fast. I am not even sure if I truly believe in what I'm preaching anymore," he thought to himself. Shawn was a ticking time bomb that was getting ready to explode.

Shawn kept seeing Donald in passing at certain church functions and their eyes would always lock. There seemed to be a mutual attraction that was unspoken between the two men. Shawn would eventually break eye contact and look away because he didn't want his lustful feeling to be obvious to others.

When there was a potluck in the reception hall, his mind was tormented. He admired how Donald ate at a nearby table. His arm muscles were popping as he devoured the fried chicken and macaroni and cheese. Connie was sitting right next to her husband and she had no idea the perverse thoughts that ran through her husband's mind.

Connie: Honey. Sister Gloria hooked up this fried chicken didn't she?

Connie's voice brought Shawn back to reality.

Shawn: Huh?

Connie repeated herself. "Sister Gloria did her thing with this fried chicken didn't she?"

Shawn: Oh yes. She is my second favorite cook next to you.

Connie's face lit up as her husband charmed her. He always knew what to say to make her smile. They ate their food. Afterward, they greeted all the church members and left.

Another time, there was a carwash fundraiser, he entertained thoughts as well. Donald was washing cars as they pulled up with the other deacons of the church. He was wearing a "wife-beater" and basketball shorts. His shirt was wet, his chest and abs could be seen as the shirt grabbed his torso.

"Donald sure looks good as he washes those cars. Oh my goodness. What am I thinking? I love my wife. Man, I am such an evil man," Shawn thought to himself.

Since Shawn was being stimulated sexually by entertaining thoughts of Donnie, he would go home every night and make love to his wife. Cassandra had no idea that her husband was thinking about a man as they had sex. Shawn was like a stallion performing pleasurable acts on his wife all night.

Connie: Oooh Baby. You are learning new tricks.

Shawn: Hmm. You are about to get it all night long.

They were like newlyweds. They couldn't keep their hands off each other. The intimacy between them was renewed. Somedays, they would come together two or three times. Shawn had a high sex drive and Connie knew it was wrong to deny him and quickly learned to enjoy it. She was glad that her husband desired her because several stories of women not being intimate with their husbands after a few years and the havoc it wreaked on their relationships had circulated. Connie did not want to lose their connection.

Some nights, she would watch Shawn sleep, pray over him, and kiss his forehead before falling to sleep. She appreciated her husband's hard work to make her happy.

"I'm a blessed woman," Connie thought. She was so happy with her husband and enjoyed the life that they shared. Eventually she would doze off to sleep. She felt like she was doing everything right in her marriage but her world was about to come crashing down. She had no idea of Shawn's internal battle.

Weeks went on and Shawn was severely tormented. The thoughts of being intimate with Donald consumed him. One day when he was at the office late in the evening. He thought that there was no one at the church. All of a sudden, the sound of the vacuum came on in the hallway and it scared him. He peeped his head out of the office to see who was cleaning and it was Donald. He felt flustered as passion consumed his loins.

Shawn: Hey there.

Donald looked up and cut off the vacuum. "Hey, there pastor."

The two men locked eyes again as they had been doing for several weeks.

Shawn: "We never really speak. We just keep staring at one another," he said as he chuckled.

Donald: Yeah, I know.

Donald smiled and laughed as well.

Shawn: You scared me because I didn't know anyone was here.

Donald: I didn't mean to scare you.

Shawn: It's okay. Well come into my office so I can get to know a little bit about you.

Donald: Okay.

Shawn went into his office and Donald followed behind him.

Shawn: Close the door and have a seat.

Donald followed the instructions.

Shawn: So how are you enjoying the church so far?

Donald: It's great. Everyone here is so nice.

Shawn: Yes, we have a great team here. Where are you from?

Donald: I'm from Atlanta.

Shawn: That's a great city. I've preached there many times.

Donald: Yes. I know. I'm a big fan. I actually moved here to be closer to you.

Shawn: Oh, yeah?

Donald: I just felt an attraction and was drawn to you.

Shawn: Wow. I heard several people tell me that before.

Shawn didn't know what kind of attraction he was talking about. So, he wanted to play it cool.

Donald: The way you move is amazing. You are a breath of fresh air.

There was an awkward silence between the two men as they read each other's body language.

Donald: Pastor, excuse me if I'm out of order but I'm a straight forward person. I see the way you look at me. Is there something you want to tell me?

Shawn couldn't believe his boldness and approach. He had to think of a response quickly so he wouldn't look guilty.

Shawn: I was looking at you because you remind me of someone that I used to know.

Donald: It's okay pastor but we both know that's not it. I feel the same way about you.

Shawn: You must be mistaken. I don't roll that way. I'm a pastor.

Donald: I know who you are. I've been with other men before and I know when someone is curious. It's all over you. You want me.

As Donald spoke, he stood up and approached Shawn. He leaned over him. Shawn stood up and the two men locked lips.

Shawn tried to resist at first but Donald had seduced him.

Donald: Don't resist.

They both undressed and began to explore one another's body. Shawn was caught up in the heat of the moment. The spirit of lust exploded in his souls as he committed an abominable act in the sight of God.

About thirty minutes later, the two men got dressed.

Shawn: I don't understand what happened. I have never done this before.

Donald: It's okay. It was destined to happen.

Shawn: I'm a married man. This was a terrible mistake. It can't happen again.

Donald: It will happen again because your wife can't satisfy you like I can. Your secret is safe with me.

Donald walks out of the office smiling. The passion quickly left. Shawn started to feel convicted, guilty, and he wanted to repent to God. However, he felt so distant from the Lord. "I'm such a hypocrite. I preach about holiness and look at me. I just slept with a man. I don't even think God would hear my prayers," he thought. The peace of the Lord he once carried now left him. He knew that the Holy Spirit was grieved by his sins. Several minutes went by as Shawn sat at his desk and shook his head in disbelief. He went to the restroom, washed up his face and private area.

"I can't leave any evidence. I don't want my wife to find out. She would be crushed if she ever found out," he thought.

Shawn locked the church and drove home. The ride home seemed like an eternity. When he went home, he kissed his wife. At dinner, his body was present but his mind was on what happened earlier. He barely touched his plate.

Connie: Honey. Are you okay?

Shawn: Huh?

Connie: Are you okay? You don't seem like yourself.

Shawn: Yes. I'm just thinking. I had a long day.

Connie: Do you want to tell me about it?

Shawn: I am just down because of sister Brenda's cancer diagnosis.

Shawn felt like he had to lie to get his wife off his back. "Oh no. Now, I'm a liar too. I'm just messing up. I tell my wife everything and now this secret is tearing me up inside," he said to himself.

Connie: That's so sad. I pray that she shall live and not die. She is one of the pillars of our church.

Shawn: I know dear. I am going to eat this later. My stomach feels funny. Please wrap up my plate.

Connie: Oh no. I pray you feel better. I knew something was wrong because lasagna is one of your favorite meals.

Shawn: Thank you. I'm going to go to bed early.

He needed some time alone to process everything. Shawn excused himself from the table. He went into the bathroom because he was feeling overwhelmed by the spirit of guilt. He washed his face and looked into the mirror. "I don't like the man that I see," he said to himself.

Shawn felt terrible. He couldn't pray because the spirit of condemnation was attacking his mind.

"You really messed up now. You aren't worthy to preach the Gospel. Just give up." Shawn was now hearing the voice of the enemy. He reluctantly agreed with the tormentor because he had no more fight. He had lost the battle and gave in to the lust of his flesh.

He felt his world collapsing down upon him. The only solution was to call it a night. Sleep would help him get his mind off the situation. He undressed and crawled into the bed. He put the warm comforter over his body. "Tomorrow, I can get a fresh start." So he thought...

CHAPTER FOUR

I GOT TO STOP

Shawn woke up with a sense of dread. It was as his heart sank in his chest as the reality of his sins played before his eyes. He rolled over in bed to see if Connie was laying next to him. She wasn't beside him and Shawn rubbed his hand along the sheets in the empty space.

"I love my wife. She doesn't deserve this."

As he thought about his wife, the smell of breakfast filled his nostrils. Suddenly his stomach started to growl. He was starving because he skipped dinner last night. He got up and went into the bathroom. He washed his face, brushed his teeth and looked in the mirror.

"I am never going to do what I did again. I am going to get myself together and it starts today. I shall walk in a new beginning," he thought to himself.

Shawn walks into the kitchen and his wife greets him with a kiss.

Shawn: Hmm. What's all this?

Shawn's mouth starts to water as he looks at the scrambled cheese eggs, buttery grits, crispy bacon, sausage patties, hash browns, biscuits with strawberry jams, orange juice, and coffee. Connie had already prepared the plates. She had her chef's apron on because cooking was her pride.

Connie: Well, since you didn't eat dinner last night I wanted to surprise you. Here is a meal that's fit for a king, my king.

Shawn: Thanks, babe. You are the best.

Shawn took his seat and began devouring the food on his plate. Connie smiled in delight.

Connie: I am so glad that you feel better. I was really worried about you.

Shawn: Yes. I feel a lot better. I have to go to the office today to prepare some sermons and work on some projects. Maybe we can cuddle later, watch a movie, then make love all night?

Connie: Hmm boy you are turning me on. Sounds like a date. I will work on my business. I have to host an event at the church next week so I need to make sure that I have enough inventory.

Shawn: It's going to be great Hun.

After breakfast, Shawn got dressed and headed out the door. He picks up the phone to call Donald.

Donald: Hello.

Shawn: Hey. How are you?

Donald: I'm good and you?

Shawn: Listen, what happened the other day was a mistake and it can never happen again.

Donald: It wasn't a mistake. We are two adults and we both wanted it. We enjoyed it.

Shawn: Look, I have so much at stake here so it can never happen again.

Donald: How about you meet me so we can talk?

Shawn: No. I don't think that will be a good idea.

Donald: Come on. I am not going to seduce you. I really do need your help with something. I need some advice. I promise it will never happen again.

Shawn: "Alright," he reluctantly agreed. He had no idea what Donald was planning.

Donald: Ok great. Meeting me at Cafe Bristol on Capital Street in 30 minutes for a cup of coffee.

Shawn: Sure.

Shawn hangs up the phone and drives over to the cafe to wait for Donald. He finds a spot on the outside patio of the restaurant. Donald shows up and the two men greet. They looked at each other awkwardly.

Donald: Listen. I apologize for what happened the other day. I don't know what came upon me.

Shawn: You are forgiven. Now what advice do you need from me?

Donald: Well, I know that you are a great writer and I want to enter a poetry contest. So I figured that you can help me.

Shawn: That's wonderful. I don't know what help I can be?

Donald: You can be a great help. You have a way of articulating words.

The waitress walks up, interrupts their conversation to ask what they wanted to drink. Shawn just asks for water because he was already stuffed from the delicious breakfast his wife prepared.

Donald: I'll take a vanilla latte to go.

Shawn: Thank you. I guess I can take a look at it.

Donald: Thank you. I actually have a copy in my car. Do you have a few minutes? I can read it to you. It's not that long.

Shawn: Ok. Just a few minutes but I have a lot of work to do today.

The waitress brings Donald his latte, he picks it up, and then leaves a tip on the table. Shawn followed Donald behind the building where his car was parked.

He gets in the passenger seat as Donald sits in the driver's seat.

Shawn: Ok I am ready.

All of a sudden, Donald leans over and kisses Shawn. At first Shawn tried to resist but the spirit of lust overtook him and he gave in. Donald began to perform oral sex on him all the while Shawn relished in the feelings. Shawn had no idea that Donald had a hidden camera in a pair of shades that were on the dash. After a few minutes, Donald let up.

Shawn: Look. This was a mistake. You tricked me. There was no poem was it?

Donald: No. I couldn't let you go. I had to have you again.

Shawn: I never want to see you again! We are finished!

Donald: You can't mean that? You just can't walk away!

Shawn: I do mean that!

Donald: If you don't give me what I want then you will be sorry.

Shawn rushes out of the car and goes to his own vehicle. He sat there for a few minutes pondering.

"How can I be so stupid? I told myself that I will never do this again. I'm not gay. I realized that I am not even attracted to Donald like I thought I was. The enemy blinded my eyes but now they are opened to my sins. I know this is wrong."

At that moment, his phone rung and it was his wife. He saw her beautiful face come across the screen but he didn't have the courage to say hello. So he ignored her call. He felt so guilty and started to feel defiled.

He went to the church, closed the door to his office, and he managed to find an old sermon from a few years ago.

"I'll just preach this tomorrow. I feel so far away from God right now. I feel dirty, unclean, and like a hypocrite. I know God will not give me a Rhema Word for His people."

As Donald was thinking these thoughts, his wife called again. He still couldn't find the strength to answer.

"How can I face her? I messed up. I broke our marital vows. I'm a disgrace in the sight of God!"

His mind was racing with thoughts of condemnation and he heard the devil speak, "You are worthless. Just admit it. You are gay. Admit it you liar!"

Shawn: No! You are a liar!

Devil: You are a failure! Everyone will find out who you really are! Just kill yourself!

Shawn: Shut up!

At that moment, Shawn had a breaking point. He put his hands on his temples, his back slid down the wall and he sat on the floor for hours until there was a knock on the door and it opened. It was his wife.

Connie: Honey. What's wrong. I called you a bunch of times and couldn't reach you. Why are you on the floor?

Shawn: "I'm sorry honey. I received a bad report. One of my old classmates passed away," he lied.

Devil: LIAR!

Shawn heard the devil in his mind yelling calling him all types of names. He tried his best to ignore the demonic chatter. However, his wife wasn't buying his excuse.

Connie: Honey, tell me what's really going on? You are so distracted.

Shawn: That's it. There is nothing else going on. Let's go home okay.

Connie: Ok. I will meet you at home in a few more hours. I have a business meeting. A local store wants to put my candles in their shop. I'm very excited about it.

Shawn: That's wonderful.

Connie: I was trying to call and tell you the great news but you weren't answering. I felt in my gut to come to check on you.

Shawn: You are such a blessing. I don't know what I would do without you.

Shawn stood up, kissed his wife and each said goodbye. During that moment, he received a text message. It was from Donald.

Donald: I enjoyed you.

Shawn texts back: Don't ever contact me again.

Donald: You don't mean that.

Shawn: Yes I do.

Donald: You belong to me now.

Shawn: You heard me.

As Shawn was about to type another text, a video popped up in the chat. As soon as he looked at it, anxiety set in. His heart pumped in his chest. It was as if the air was being squeezed out of his lungs. The video was a recording of their sexual encounter in Donald's car. It was clear that Shawn was receiving oral sex from him and he couldn't deny it.

Shawn: What is this?

Donald: If you don't do what I want then the world will see this.

Shawn: What do you want? I can give you money. I'll get you a car or house. Anything. Please don't show anyone. Delete it, please.

Donald: I don't want all that. All I want is you.

Shawn: What do you mean all you want is me? I'm married.

Donald: Sadly, I know. I want to see you every week or you will be sorry.

Shawn: Ok. I'll do anything just promise me that you will delete it.

Donald: I promised. See you next week. The same location. At the same time.

Shawn: Ok.

"What have I gotten myself into? I'm ruined. This was supposed to be a one time thing but now it's a living hell."

Shawn began to weep but managed to get himself together. Later that night, he watched a movie with Connie but his mind wasn't there. Even though they were cuddled up, he couldn't stop thinking about how he was going to get out of this mess with Donald.

"Maybe I will hire a hitman. No that will never work. Maybe, I will poison him. No that will never work. Maybe, I will strangle him myself. No. What am I doing? I'm not a murder."

Connie: You enjoying the movie babe?"

Shawn: Huh?

He heard his wife ask a question but was too distracted by his thoughts to clearly hear what she asked.

Connie: Do you like the movie?

Shawn: "Oh yes," he lied.

Shawn didn't like the person he was becoming. He couldn't pray, read his word, and be honest with his wife. He was an adulterer, liar, murder, and hypocrite. Later that night, Shawn barely could perform in the bedroom. He pleasured his wife and made up an excuse for why he didn't want to make love. The truth was that he couldn't get an erection because he was stressed out.

Connie: Thank you baby for taking care of me. Now let's finish.

Shawn: No. Tonight was all about you.

Connie: Ok baby.

Connie felt this to be odd because usually her husband wanted to make love all through the night. "I guess he has a lot on his plate," she thought. Then she drifted off to sleep. Shawn had a hard time sleeping. Thoughts of revenge filled his mind. "I gotta get that video even if it costs me everything."

The next day, Shawn had to preach for Wednesday night service. It was one of the hardest things he ever had to do. As he preached his old sermon, the devil's voice rang loud in his head, "They will never listen to a liar like you."

Shawn ignored the enemy's voice but then he locked eyes with Donald in the crowd. "Why is he even here?" he thought. Donald held up his phone as a reminder of their earlier conversation. The spirit of intimidation came upon Shawn.

Suddenly the video clip resurfaced in his mind. Beads of sweat started dripping off his forehead. His stomach churned as a nauseous feeling hit it. Shawn started to fumble on some words and people started to look at each other as they wondered if the pastor was okay.

Shawn: When...when...when...when...uhmm uhmm uhmm...the Lord makes a promise...uhmm uhmm.. He will...hmm...hmmm.. He will...do it.

Despite the distractions, Shawn was able to pull off preaching the sermon and the crowd erupted with praising God for His goodness. Connie knew that her husband's behavior was off and she vowed to find out the dark secret that he was carrying.

CHAPTER FIVE

THE RAMPAGE

Donald was a complex man. He lived a life full of rejection. His mother Lorraine would get drunk and say, "I wish you were a girl." All his life, he yearned for his mother's affection yet he failed to realize that he would never be good enough. As a child, seeds of perversion we're planted in his mind. Donald loved his mother and wanted to please her so he would go into his mother's closet and try on her high heels. He feared that if he got caught then she would beat him. When she found her son trying on her shoes one day, she felt a sense of satisfaction and smiled. Donald took that as a sign of approval.

Lorraine dreamed of having a little girl so she could dress her up like a princess. When she found out that she was pregnant and didn't know who the father was she began to hate all men. When Donald was born Lorraine dressed him in pink onesies, pajamas, and frilly dresses until he was three years old. His hair was long and many people often mistook him for a girl during outings with his mom.

Donald felt that he wasn't good enough and began looking for affections elsewhere. During his teenage years, his mother started dating a pastor named Michael. He was always kind to Donald and made him feel accepted. This is where his obsession began with pastors. He wanted to be like his mother and enjoy the same things even men. The courtship didn't work out between Lorraine and Michael because of Lorraine's emotional instability. However, she would always date a man in the church because she felt they wouldn't play games like the men did in the clubs. She knew that a church man was ready to settle down and get married. Lorraine finally hit gold. She married an older church deacon twenty years her senior and they had a daughter.

Donald didn't get along with his stepfather too well. However, they tolerated each other. During the weekends, Donald would visit the Rainbow Club and dress in drag. He was embraced by the LGBTQ+ community there. This was the only place he felt comfortable expressing himself. He had plenty of practice putting on makeup and wigs. He would look in the mirror and say, "These chicks don't have nothing on me, honey." His stepfather disapproved of his lifestyle so he would sneak around behind his back to dress in drag.

Donald spent his school years being in the closet. He went out with a few girls as a cover-up but never showed any real interest in them. He was always the homeboy type of best friend to these girls. There wasn't any attraction on his part. One day, a girl named Merlenda, who he was dating, tried to kiss him and he ducked. She got very upset because he refused to make-out with her and the two broke up.

Donald would mess around with some football players at his school but they threaten to beat him up if he ever told someone what they did. He would go over their houses when the parents were away or sometimes they told the parents they were going to do homework after school. Donald began to feel used and grew tired of being alone. He desired a relationship and was searching for love. One day out of boredom he flipped on the television. He couldn't find anything that interested him. After flipping the channel for a while, he saw a man that looked similar to Michael the pastor who dated his mother years ago.

Their complexions, smiles, and height we're similar. Donald's heart fluttered with hope as the television now had his full attention. This was the first time Donald laid eyes on Shawn Wayne. Pastor Shawn was a guest on a popular Christian network. Donald fell instantly in love and head over heels. He searched out Shawn's information on the internet and found out that he was going to be preaching in a city near him in a few weeks.

Donald was so happy. He began to fantasize about Shawn. He created a secret scrapbook full of pictures of Shawn. He would draw hearts and kisses all over them. He hid this scrapbook in the back of his closet so his parents couldn't find it. From that day on, Donald made a vow that he would wait for his true love, Shawn. When the football players wanted to mess around after school Donald would say, "I can't anymore. My true love wouldn't appreciate that." He would then smile and walk away.

Donald thought about Shawn all day. He would write love letters to him and keep them in a shoebox in his closet.

"Dear love. Your smile brightens up my day. You are a breath of fresh air. You looked so good today. I am falling deeper in love with you. Soon we will be face to face. I pray the feeling is mutual."

"-yours truly."

Donald started doing pushups and sit-ups in preparation to meet Shawn at his meeting. He brought a brand new suit because he wanted to look his best when he went to this event. The night finally came for the revival and Donald made sure he sat up front. The meeting was packed. As Shawn preached a message, Donald fantasized about their future. During a few seconds during the message Shawn looked at Donald then looked away and finished his sermon. Donald ran with those few seconds of eye contact and the infatuation grew.

Weeks later, as Donald was watching Shawn's marriage video announcement. At that moment, sorrow filled his heart.

"No. No. No! You can't! You are mine!" He slammed his fists into the wall and punched a huge hole into it. He made up his mind that day to get what he thought belonged to him.

A few years past and Donald moved out of his parent's house. He tried to date men that looked like Shawn but he wasn't happy. He would use these men and kick them to the curb. Donald had an extra bedroom that he always kept locked. No one was allowed in it. Many of his lovers inquired about this room but Donald would always tell them not to worry about that.

Inside this room was a shrine to Shawn. The walls were covered with pictures of him. There was an x on Connie's face on some photos. Also, Donald cut out his body from some pictures and glued it on top of images with Shawn by placing his body next to his.

Donald made sure to move down the street from Shawn's church. Every time he saw him, he made sure to make eye contact with him. He would secretly follow Shawn home, stalk him, and even enter his garage sitting in his car. The extent of his obsession knew no bounds.

One day he followed Shawn to the church. He knew no one was supposed to be there. While the pastor was in his office, Donald had to make his move. He had to get his attention, so he took out a vacuum and started vacuuming outside of Shawn's office. When the pastor came out, he knew it was time to seduce him. After the sexual encounter in the office, he rejoiced. He went home into his shrine room and wrote a love letter.

> "Dear Love. Finally, we locked embraces and explored each other. Passion was ignited as we pleased one another. I know you enjoyed me as much as I enjoyed you. I'm looking forward to spending a lifetime with you."
>
> — Your Only True Love

When he finished the letter, he put it in his shoebox. He went out of the room and locked the door behind him with his key. Donald knew that Shawn might hesitate to leave his wife so he wanted to level the playing field. He took a pair of shades that had a camera inside and put it on his dash in his car. He determined that the next time he and Shawn got together, he would record it so he could always treasure that moment as he watched it.

Even though Donald was successful at seducing the pastor there was a problem and her name was

Connie. He knew that as long as she was in the picture he could never fully be with his true love.

"Connie, your time is up! You must go!" he declared. Now his plan for elimination was now in full effect.

CHAPTER SIX

REVENGE

Today was the big day of Connie's church event. For the past several weeks she had been making a variety of candles. Some candles we're scented and the aromas ranged from pumpkin spice, cinnamon, peppermint oil, Hawaiian breeze, honey blossom, summer rain, cherry limeade, coconut passion, and a dozen more fragrances. She had four big crates of products that she needed to take to the church. It was early in the morning. She hadn't showered or ate breakfast.

Connie: Honey, I have finished loading up the crates. Can you please put them in the back of the van. I will have some people at the church help me unload and set up.

Shawn: Ok dear.

Shawn looked at all the crates in amazement.

Shawn: Whoa. I can't believe you did all this by yourself. You are one talented lady.

Shawn walked over to Connie and she smiled. They kissed and loaded up the van. They drove to the church together and were greeted by some deacons and their wives. Everyone was helpful as they brought the candles inside and set up the product tables.

The presentation was beautiful. The banquet hall had twelve tables that we're draped with a Burgundy cloth with a sign going across that said Connie's Creations. The candles were separated in different groups: the spring collection, fall collection, summertime collection, winter collection, fruit collection, blossom collection, fantasy collection, faith collection, Christmas collection, soy collection, Easter collection, and tropical collection. Each collection had its own set up on one of the tables. There was a beautiful banner with Connie's name and logo.

When everything was finished setting up, everyone was ready to go home to get dressed because the event wasn't for another 4 more hours.

Connie: Thank you everyone. I will see everyone at 1 pm.

Everyone greeted each other bye and left. About 30 minutes later, a man dressed in all black arrived on the scenes. He had a black ski mask on and he picked the locks on the door to gain entry. He knew the security code so he entered the pin before it could notify the authorities with the destination time frame. This man was Donald and he had one thing on his mind which was to destroy Connie.

He entered the banquet hall and saw how lovely the room looked. He immediately started turning over tables, throwing candles across the room, slicing the table cloths and banner with his pocket knife. Glass was everywhere as the jars burst upon impact when they were thrown against the wall. The room looked as if a tornado hit it. Donald felt a sense of satisfaction as he viewed the destruction he caused.

Suddenly he heard a sound so he leaned up against the wall trying to hide behind the door. Two women were entering the church carrying food. One had a cake and the other had a pan of roast. They were talking about everything that needed to be done.

Betsy: They were setting up this morning. Let's go see it.

Annette: Ok let's put this food down on a table in the banquet hall.

At that moment, Donald's eyes got wide with the fear of getting caught. The door of the room opened and the women gasped at the mess.

Women: Oh no. What happened?

Donald came out of hiding and rushed into the two women as he tackled them down to the ground. They fell on top of one another as the cake went flying across the room and the pot roast was all over the floor. The hot liquid of carrots, onions, potatoes, and beef made contact with their skin. They moaned in pain as they tried to gain their composure but by that time Donald was already out the door and driving down the street.

Betsy: Call the police

Annette: Ok. I'll call pastor.

Shawn and Connie were both getting dressed when Shawn's phone rang. Connie was wearing a beautiful flowing spring dress that complimented her curves.

Shawn was wearing his favorite polo shirt along with a pair of starched jeans. Shawn was spraying his favorite cologne and Connie was finishing up her hair.

Shawn: Hello.

Annette: Hello Pastor. This is Annette. Someone broke into the church, attacked Betsy and me, and destroyed all of the first lady's candles.

Shawn: Are you for real?

Annette: Yes.

Shawn: Call the police. We are on our way.

Annette: Okay. The police are on their way.

Shawn hung up the phone with a look of disbelief on his face. He looked at his wife.

Shawn: Babe. We have to leave right now. Annette and Betsy were attacked. Someone broke into the church and they destroyed your candles.

Connie: Oh no. All my hard work was for nothing.

Shawn: Babe that is not true. The Lord birthed greatness out of you. You can do the event again. The next time we will have security guards.

Connie laid her head in her husband's chest and he held her momentarily as she wept.

Shawn: Let's go. They are waiting for us.

When they arrived at the church, the police were at the scene trying to collect any evidence. Two detectives walked up to Shawn and his wife.

Detective Black: Hello. I'm detective Black and this is my partner Detective Sky.

Shawn: Hello. Nice to meet you. I am the pastor here and this is my wife.

They both extended their hands to give them a handshake.

Detective Sky: Do you have any idea who could have done this?

Connie: No.

Detective Black: What about you Sir?

Shawn: No.

Detective Sky: Do you have any enemies?

At that moment, Donald came to Shawn's mind. "He wouldn't have done this. He couldn't be that crazy," he thought. The detectives looked at Shawn because they could tell that he knew something that he was saying.

Detective Black: Sir is there something that you need to tell us. Withholding evidence is a crime.

Shawn: There is nothing that I know. I want to find out who did this as much as you want to.

Detective Sky: Very well. If you find out something then give us a call.

The detectives handed Shawn and Connie their business cards and proceeded to walk off.

Connie: Is that it? No arrest. No evidence.

Detective Black: Mam. We have one of our experts dusting for prints. We will be in touch.

As the two detectives walked off the scene they looked at each other and chatted.

Detective Sky: That husband knows more than he is telling us.

Detective Black: Let's keep a close eye on him.

Annette and Betsy were sitting in the back of the ambulance that was on the scene. The pot roast caused burns on their legs when they were tackled. Blisters started to form. Also they were hurt from being rushed by the perpetrator. Shawn and Connie went over to the Ambulance to check on the ladies and then they went inside to see the damage. As they viewed the broken candles and destroyed banner, Connie cried hysterically.

Connie: Oh no! Why! Who would do such an evil thing?"

Shawn was lost for words. The only thing that he could do was to hold his wife. He knew that he had to be strong. Shawn called one of the deacons at the church and told him to call as many people to get the word out that the event at 1 pm was canceled. He took distraught Connie home and they got some rest. That night, Donald drove down the street from the pastor's house. He sat outside as he viewed the house.

He texted Shawn repeatedly throughout the day but no response. "I know he isn't ignoring my texts," he thought. The idea infuriated him.

Text 1: Hey there.

Five minutes go by.

Text 2: Hello?

Fifteen minutes go by.

Text 3: I'm having a great day. How about you?

Another five minutes past.

Text 4: I know you aren't ignoring me? Remember what we promised?

Twenty minutes later.

Text 5: I will ruin you! You are about to lose everything!

Ten minutes later.

Text 6: I am sorry about that last message. I didn't mean it. I love you.

One hour later.

Text 7: Hey. Give me a call. I need to talk to you about something.

Five minutes later.

Text 8: I really do need your advice. Please give me a call.

Fifteen minutes later.

Text 9: Are you okay? It's not like you not to answer your phone.

Two minutes later.

Text 10: Answer me please. I'm worried. I've got a surprise for you.

Thirty minutes later.

Text 11: Ok. Evidently you are too busy for me. You are a liar. I hate you.

One minute later.

Text 12: I didn't mean that. You are the best thing that happened to me.

Three minutes later.

Text 13: I love you. Say it back. I can't wait to see you this week.

Twenty minutes later.

Shawn's phone was downstairs on the kitchen counter while he was upstairs with his wife consoling her. Since Donald was so upset, he got out of the car and crept up to the house. He took out a blade and began to key Connie's car.

HE IS MINE!

He engraved these words right along the side of her black sedan then he went into his car and sped off. The next morning, Shawn went downstairs into the kitchen. He wanted to do something nice for his wife so he decided to cook a nice breakfast. He noticed his cellphone and saw that he had a ton of messages from members of the church checking on him and his wife. Then he saw messages from Donald. When he saw all the crazy messages, he felt a pit in the bottom of his stomach. Anxiety started to set in. He started to hyperventilate and he crouched down on the floor to get himself together. He noticed that the trash can was full so he took out the old bag and headed outside to throw it away in the trash can. "I just need some fresh air," he thought. As Shawn walked outside his eyes fell upon his wife's car.

Shawn: What in the world?

Immediately, he knew that Donald was responsible for everything that had happened. He threw the garbage away. Got his phone from the counter and went back outside to make a call.

Donald: Hello my love.

Shawn: I'm not anything to you. If you come near me or my family again then I will kill you. Do you understand?

Donald: What are you talking about?

Shawn: I know you were the one behind the candles and now you messed with my wife's car.

Donald: Let me remind you of our little arrangement and what's on the line.

Shawn: Forget that. It will never happen. I don't care what you do. Stay out of my life.

Donald: You will be sorry for this.

Donald hung up the phone. He paced back and forth in his living room. "No! No! No!" he yelled! "I've worked all of my life to find you and now your wife is ruining everything!" He paces the floor some more and then he receives an idea which would bring Shawn to his demise. He pulled up the video on his laptop of their sexual encounter and viewed it. Rage engulfed him. "I will give you one more chance. If you don't do what I want then this video goes viral," he said out loud. Donald got in his car to go stalk Shawn again. He pulled up down the street from his house out of view so he could be closer to Shawn.

After the phone call with Donald, Shawn stormed back into the house. He hated to tell his wife more bad news. He didn't want to tell her that he had slept with a man that's psycho and now he is trying to destroy their marriage. He knew that if she ever found out then she would leave him. Connie was still in bed when he walked into the room.

Shawn: Honey. You won't believe this but someone keyed your car. I am going to find out who it is and kill them.

Connie: What? You will not do such a thing because you will be in prison for life. That's it. I'm calling the police.

Connie picks up the phone and calls one of the detectives that she met yesterday. An hour later they arrived at their house to take a statement and to ask questions. Connie put on her robe and went outside to view the damage to her vehicle. Shawn followed behind her. She immediately started to suspect her husband of cheating but didn't want to accuse him without having the facts. "This must be a jealous female trying to steal my man, " she thought.

Detective Sky: Hello again. The police couldn't find any evidence at the church.

Connie: They couldn't?

Detective Black: I have a feeling that these two crimes are related.

Detective Sky: I am going to ask you again. Do you have any enemies or is there anyone that you could think of that could've done this?

Connie: No. Everyone loves my husband and I. We treat everyone kindly in our community.

Detective Black: Mr. Wayne. Is there something that you know here? You look like you are hiding something.

Shawn: Excuse me? Why don't you find the person who is out to get us instead of blaming me?

Detective Sky: We will have an officer to sit outside your house and at your church for a few days.

Connie: Ok. Thank you.

Shawn puts his arm around his wife to hold her as they stood in the driveway talking to the detectives. When Donald saw this vengeance gripped him. At that moment, he lost it. He slammed his fists hard into the steering wheel repeatedly. "No! No! No!" he yelled. He began to cry as he realized that his true love was slipping out of his grasp. He drove away from the scene. He came home and went straight to his laptop. He pulled up the sex video and started to download it to various websites. "I told you not to mess with me. You are out of chances." He grabbed his key in a rage and unlocked the door to his shrine room. He walked up to one of the photos of Shawn and drew a big black x on his face. "If I can't have you then nobody will!" he exclaimed.

CHAPTER SEVEN

SOMETHING ISN'T RIGHT

Over the next few days, Connie noticed a change in her husband. He wasn't his usual self, and there was friction in their marriage. They never argued, but now it seemed like that's all they did. The day after her car was keyed, her husband was snappy. He seemed to have a short-fuse. Connie walked up behind him in the kitchen, and he jumped.

Shawn: Don't sneak up on me like that!

Connie: I'm sorry.

She walked away because he was a patient man, not a mean one. She knew she didn't deserve to be yelled at but she figured that he was stressed because of everything that was happening.

Another time, Shawn was in the living room, and he seemed to be in deep thought. He didn't even notice her when she walked into the room. She wanted to see if he wanted something to drink. She had just prepared some ice tea.

Connie: Honey. Honey.

She waved her hands in his face at a distance trying to get his attention because he seemed to look right through her.

Shawn: What?!

Connie was a bit taken back. She didn't even recognize her husband. It was as if a demonic spirit spoke through him.

Connie: I didn't mean to startle you. I was just asking if you wanted something to drink.

Shawn: No!

She walked out of the room and went to her bedroom to pray. "Lord, I bind up this demonic spirit inside my husband in Jesus' name."

She stood to her feet and exclaimed, "Satan! You can't have my marriage!"

Connie felt like she was walking on eggshells. Anything ticked her husband off, and she was tired of it. She didn't realize that her husband's sins we're now catching up to him. He was overwhelmed with guilt, anxiety, and severely harassed by the devil in his mind.

Shawn would lock himself in his study and rock back and forth. His body would convulse, and he would sweat. He took some pills for the anxiety he felt, but it didn't stop the devil from tormenting him.

"LIAR! LIAR! LIAR!" said the tormentor.

Shawn couldn't seem to get free! There was no joy or peace for Shawn. Donald's threats replayed in his mind. He felt like he was the reason his wife's business and car were damaged. The burden of the secret ate away at this soul. He was restless and shut down. He pushed his wife away and withdrew from everyone as the spirit of heaviness slowly sucked the life out of him. He put someone else in charge of the church because he couldn't bear to look at the people's faces as he preached.

"They know what I did," he thought. I know someone is going to find out. He felt better avoiding everyone. He fell into a deep depression. The devil had Shawn exactly where he wanted him, which was in isolation.

Connie needed her husband more than anything else. She was scared and started to blame herself for what was going on. She grew weary of her husband not being in bed at night. She went to bed by herself and woke up alone. She missed her husband holding her in his arms. She enjoyed his kisses along her back and neck. She yearned for his touch and needed his conversation.

They used to share the highlights of each other's day, but now it was nothing. It was as if the two lovers now became strangers living underneath the same roof.

Shawn would stay up late at night as he made excuses that he needed to clear his mind. He was afraid that Donald would try something again and wanted to catch him in the act. He was mad enough to kill him.

One day Connie woke up and checked the time. It was past midnight and her husband wasn't beside her. She went downstairs and saw her husband looking out the blinds.

Connie: Honey, is everything alright.

Shawn: Yes, everything is fine.

Connie: Is there someone out there?

Shawn: No. I'm going to make sure of it.

Connie: Are you going to come to bed?

Shawn: Yes. I will be there later.

Connie walked back upstairs and laid there. She waited for her husband. An hour went by, and he still was downstairs. Connie drifted off to sleep, and when she woke up in the morning, the spot beside her was empty. Her husband never came to bed. Shawn had fallen asleep on the sofa downstairs.

Connie noticed that Shawn picked over his food during lunchtime and then again at dinner. For lunch, she prepared him burgers and sweet potato fries. For dinner, she made meatloaf, mashed potatoes with gravy, and peas. She didn't say anything about him picking at his food at lunch, but she had to at dinner. He barely spoke to her, and being around him was awkward. They sat in silence for a few minutes at the table and she watched him push the peas around on his plate.

Connie: Babe, is there something you need to tell me?

Shawn: No.

Connie: You are acting differently. Please don't shut me out.

At that moment, she placed her hand on top of his but he pulled away. Connie was hurt. The lack of communication was crushing her. She fought back tears and erupted in anger.

Connie: I'm your wife! You treat me like a total stranger! I am not the one to blame here!

Shawn: I'm sorry. I know you aren't.

Connie: Why can't you trust me? There shouldn't be any secrets between us.

Shawn didn't even respond to her outburst. He was cold and affectionless.

She wanted to slap him across the face at that moment as a way to cause him to come back to reality. However, she resisted the urge and walked away.

Connie felt like someone stabbed her in her heart. She loved her husband and wanted to fight for her marriage. Later, she cleaned off the dinner table. Shawn had already left the room. "I know what I can do," she thought. "I'll dress up in some sexy lingerie. He will want me then."

Connie went upstairs, showered, and shaved. While wrapped in a towel, She pinned her hair up in an updo. She took body oil and rubbed it all over herself. She knew that the secret to soft skin was oil. Then she took the perfume that was her husband's favorite scent on her and put some on her neck, wrists, and inner thighs.

She went to her dresser and pulled out a lacey red teddy and a matching G-string. She put it on and admired her body in the mirror. She wanted to make sure everything fit perfectly to gain her husband's approval. "Shawn is going to like this," she said to herself and smiled.

She realized that she wasn't done yet. She put on a garter belt and some red stilettos. Then she walked down the hall and into her husband's study room.

Shawn sat at the desk and didn't notice her at first as she stood in the doorway so she cleared her throat. He looked up and his eyes widened.

Shawn: Wow!

Connie knew she hit the jackpot as she now had his full attention. She walks seductively over to her husband and kissed him. She took off her underwear and tossed it across the room.

Shawn: Honey. Not right now.

Shawn tried to resist but Connie wouldn't give up.

Connie: I'm not taking no for an answer. We haven't made love in days.

Connie sat on the desk and her husband stood up. She pulled down her husband's pants, grabbed his waist, and forced his love into hers. She could tell that his mind was somewhere else the whole time so she stopped him. She was so disappointed that she left and went to the bathroom. She shut the door and cried.

"Something isn't right," she sobbed.

Shawn and Connie had a great sex life. It was full of passion and he always made her feel desired. This was the first time in their marriage that she felt unwanted. She wiped the tears away and blew her nose. She changed into her pajamas then laid in the empty bed. She silently cried herself to sleep.

The next morning, Connie was sitting at the table drinking coffee when Shawn walked into the room.

Shawn: Good morning.

He leaned over Connie and kissed her. He seemed to be his normal self again. Connie wasn't buying it. She knew something wasn't right. The lack of affection, no communication, not eating, not sleeping in the bed, lack of intimacy, and fits of anger were all adding up.

Connie: Morning.

There was a sense of heartbreak in her response. Sadly, Shawn was too consumed in his own world to notice.

Connie didn't know how to feel. She had just cried herself to sleep after a failed attempt at intimacy. It was as if she was making love to an inanimate object. No feeling or passion involved.

Shawn: Can you make me some coffee? I'm going to shower and head to the church office to prepare for the conference this weekend.

Connie: Sure.

Shawn put his phone on the counter and headed upstairs. As soon as she was in the clear, she searched his phone. She went through the emails, texts, and social media messages, but she couldn't find anything.

"Maybe I am just overreacting. If he was cheating on me then why leave his phone here in the open for me to find something?" She thought.

Ten minutes later, as she was pouring a cup of coffee, Shawn came into the room and grabbed it. He sat down and drank most of it before heading out. Connie gave him his space. She didn't know what to say to him without having an emotional outburst.

"When I speak my mind I get nothing from him," she said to herself. "I need to talk to someone before I lose it."

She picks up the phone and dials her best friend Lisa Green. Lisa is an intercessor and very discerning.

Lisa: Hello.

Connie: Hey gurl.

Lisa: Hey. What's going on?

Connie: Well...

Lisa: Look before you say something, the Lord had me up all night praying for you and your husband. I can see the devil trying to cause marital strife. I feel sorrow and pain every time I pray for you guys. I can't shake it. Are you guys ok?

Connie: No.

Connie burst into tears. Lisa has a prophetic gift and those words were right on.

Connie: I'm tired sis. First my business and car were attacked and now my marriage. I feel defeated. I worked for weeks making candles that were destroyed. Someone broke into the church and sabotaged my event. My husband won't touch me, communicate, or even sleep in the same bed. I can barely pray. I just need strength.

Lisa: I am so sorry. You will get past this. I wasn't going to say anything but how long have you known me.

Connie: Since middle school.

Lisa: Has the prophetic anointing on my life ever been wrong?

Connie: No.

Lisa: Remember I told you that I had a dream that sister Barbara was going to die and she did?

Connie: Yes.

Lisa: Remember when I told you that lady was doing witchcraft and praying against the ministry and you found out that she was?

Connie: Yes. Why all the questions?

Lisa: You are my best friend. We are closer than sisters. I will always tell you the truth. I love you more than life. I hate to see you hurting. I try to stay out of married people's business but as I prayed for your husband, I kept hearing the word, "Adulterer."

Connie: What?

Lisa: I wasn't going to say anything but you need to know the truth and the reason for Shawn's behavior. There is someone else in the picture just ask your husband.

Connie was a bit taken back. "No. Not Shawn. He loves me."

But then reality set in. "Well things haven't been the best between us," she thought. Connie grew silent as she thought about everything and how it all started to make sense.

Lisa: Hello?

Connie: Thanks for the information. I will call you back.

All day Connie wrestled with the idea of her husband being an adulterer. She cried then got angry then pulled herself together. It seemed like this cycle continued until she heard her husband walk through the door. Distraught, hair out of place, and makeup smeared she met him in the living room. Shawn looked surprised because he could tell that she had been crying.

Shawn: What's wrong?

Connie: We need to talk. I know about the other person.

At that moment, the color disappeared out of Shawn as dread gripped him. He sat down and looked in a daze. The thing he feared the most came upon him. The secret was eating him up inside and had taken its toll.

Shawn: I'm so sorry. I don't even know where to begin.

Connie: Start at the beginning.

CHAPTER EIGHT

EXPOSURE

Shawn couldn't look his wife in the eyes because he knew that he was responsible for her pain. "I really screwed up," he thought as he swallowed down the taste of bile. He took a deep breath before he started from the beginning.

Shawn: I am so sorry. I never meant to hurt you. I have been dealing with my demons for far too long. You don't deserve to be in the dark. It all started when I was a boy.

He paused because he was ashamed of what he was about to say next. He never shared this part of his past with anyone.

Connie: Go ahead. I'm listening.

She fought back tears and her throat burned with anguish.

Shawn: Well. I was raped when I was around five years old by an older boy. My father invited his mistress over with her son while my mother went to work one day. They were in the back room fooling around and the son beat me up and raped me. My father never came to check on me. Instead he passed out on the couch in the living because he got drunk. I laid on the floor for hours, hurt, and violated until my mother came home from work. She knew what happened and she loved me through it. A few days later, my father died in a car accident.

Shawn paused again because as he told this story, he re-lived the pain. He realized he was carrying a wound that never properly healed.

Connie: Wow! I'm so sorry.

She tried to be sensitive to her husband even though she was angry and hurt.

Shawn: My mother blamed herself for my father's death and she died with that guilt. I struggled with my sexuality for years but since I was a minister I never explored it.

He exhales as he gains strength to say what was coming next. "Confused about his sexuality?" Connie thought.

Shawn: There was a guy at the church named Donald. He seduced me one day in my office and it only happened once.

Shawn lied to his wife because he didn't want to hurt her anymore.

Connie: What?! You slept with a man! How can I compete with that!

Shawn: I know. I know. I'm so sorry.

Connie: And you violated the House of God! How could you?

Connie was fuming. She began to pace the floor.

Connie: I gave you my life. I loved you. I treated you like a King. All for what? For you to throw it all away!

Shawn: Babe. It will never happen again. I told him it was a mistake and to leave us alone.

Connie: Leave us alone? Wait! Was he the one responsible for the candles and my car?

Shawn: Yes.

Connie: Hold up! You knew that this man destroyed my property and did nothing.

Shawn: It's not like that. I threatened him and I didn't know until recently.

Connie: I'm calling the police. He needs to pay for what he did.

Shawn was lost for words. He didn't know what to say to his wife to console her. He knew that he had messed up big time.

Connie: Don't even look at me! After this conference, we are through!

Connie stormed out of the room. Shawn put his hands on his forehead and exhaled. He could feel the anxiety coming back again.

The next day, the detectives knocked on Donald's door. No one answered. They had obtained a warrant to search the property and they were prepared to make an arrest. They kicked down the door and looked everywhere. They realized that one door in the house was locked so they kicked it open. They stood in disbelief. They couldn't believe that the walls were full of photos of Shawn. They noticed that some photos had Donald next to them. Other photos had Connie's face crossed out!

Detective Sky: Wow!

Detective Black: We know who is responsible for the attacks.

Donald was driving back home and as he got closer to his house, he saw the police car in his driveway. He stopped driving, put his car in reverse, and took off.

Donald: I have to stay low. The police are looking for me.

Donald drove two hours away and got a cheap motel. He was cautious and used cash to pay for the room. He knew if he swiped his debit card they would track him down. He needed to go somewhere to think and process everything.

The next day, Connie went to the grocery store. She needed to get out of the house and keep her mind off things. She still loved her husband and was pondering giving him another chance. As soon as she walked in people began to stare at her. At first, she didn't notice it but then it became obvious. "They must know that my husband cheated on me," she thought. "I feel like such a fool." She parked the basket in the aisle and rushed out of the store. She ran to her husband's car and wept. She hadn't gotten her car painted yet. She didn't want anyone to see the words 'HE IS MINE' on the side of her car. After she got herself together, she left for home. When she walked through the door, Shawn met her in the hallway.

Shawn: I know you don't want to talk to me but I want you to give me another chance. I love you. I need you by my side.

Connie: You know people were staring at me today in the store like they knew you were a cheater. I don't know if I can give you another chance. Give me time.

"Oh no. Maybe Donald did show people the video. I have to make sure my wife never finds out, "Shawn thought to himself.

Connie walked pass Shawn into the bedroom and shut the door. Shawn had been sleeping on the couch. Tomorrow was the day of the conference. People were coming from all over the United States, so he thought. He had no idea that video of him receiving oral sex was starting to gain traction on the internet. He couldn't focus on what he was going to speak on. He hadn't heard the voice of God for weeks nor had he felt His presence. Shawn felt lost. "I guess I will have to fake it til I make it," he thought. "I'm pretty sure that I can preach out of my gift. I know I will get past this and get back in right standing with God."

That night, Donald drove back into town. He knew that tomorrow was the day of the conference. He was full of vengeance and he wasn't satisfied that the event was still going forward. He pulled around the back of the church and breaks a window. He climbed through and went into the media booth where the equipment for LIVE streaming was located. He inserted a usb into the side of the laptop and imported a file named, "Conference File." This file was really the sex video. It had a thumbnail of the photo of the church so it could be disguised. Then he took out the usb and placed it in his pocket.

Next, Donald went into the pastor's office and logged onto his computer. He opened up Shawn's email and looked through the contacts until he found all the people that he knew were on the media team. He typed their names in the send line and typed a message.

"Please make sure that you LIVE stream the file that was downloaded last night named Conference File. It is a surprise to my wife and for those in attendance. Don't press play until after worship. Thank you."

— Pastor Shawn

Donald sent the email and exited the program. Then he crawled out the broken window. He spent a night in his car down the street from the church. He planned to see everything unravel the next day.

The next day, the car ride with Shawn and Connie was silent. The tension between them was thick. They didn't want anyone to find out what they were going through. They wanted people to receive what they needed from God.

When they arrived, they noticed that the parking lot was half full which was odd because the event is usually packed hours in advance. When they walked into the church, some people were looking at them because they heard about the rumors of the sex video. However, they didn't want to believe it and wanted to give Pastor Shawn the opportunity to address it. Pastor Shawn had no idea that the sex video was viral on the internet.

Pastor Shawn and Connie sat in their seats on the pulpit. The worship team began to sing and when they finished they took their seat in the pew. Next the media team hit play on the video per the instructions in the email. A picture of the thumbnail of the church was shown on the projector. All of a sudden, was the video of Shawn sitting in the passenger seat with his eyes rolled back in his head as he moaned in pleasure. However the person that was pleasuring him wasn't his wife but Donald.

As the video played, everyone gasped and was shocked. Connie was in disbelief. "I think I'm about to be sick," she said as she covered her mouth and rushed out of the sanctuary to vomit.

Shawn stood up. "Cut that off! Cut it off!"

Someone on the media team hit stop.

Shawn: Look! I humble myself right now and I apologize. I have brought shame to God and to you as your pastor. I fell. I sinned against God and against you. I pray that you will find it in your heart to forgive me so we can move forward.

As he was speaking, some people got up and smacked their teeth and walked out. Others sat in their seat in disbelief.

Shawn gave the microphone to one of the deacons and he took over.

Deacon Brown: Come on everybody. The night isn't over. Let's get what we came here for. Amen.

Shawn didn't know what else to do so he walked to his car and waited for his wife to come out of the building. That's when he heard the gunshots.

FIVE MINUTES EARLIER

Donald sat in his car up the street from the church. He knew this was the big reveal of the sex video. Shawn couldn't run from what he did. "I can't wait to see the look on people's faces," he thought and smiled sadistically. He could already tell that Shawn's demise was near because the parking lot wasn't packed. He knew that the video was going viral on the internet. He wanted Connie to be out of the picture permanently. So he felt like he had no other option but to expose Shawn. He figured that he could be with

Shawn later once everything dies down. He hoped that they could move somewhere and get a fresh start.

Donald watched as people left the church and got in their cars to drive off. He looked at his watch. "The service just started so I know that the video must've been played." He began to chuckle. He put his seat back and laid back for a minute. He wanted to bask in his victory. Then he heard a knock on his window.

He sat up and looked out the window to stare down the barrel of a magnum 365.

Pop! Pop! Pop!

The shooter was dressed in all black and ran off. Donald was shot in the head, neck, and chest. He died instantly. He fell over dead leaning towards the passenger seat as blood oozed out his body and brain matter splattered all across the dash and windshield.

When Shawn heard the gunshots, he didn't know what direction it came from.

"Oh no! Is someone shooting in the church," he thought. Suddenly he realized that the sound of the gunshots didn't come from the inside but the outside because it was very loud. He put his hand on his brow as he scoped out his surroundings. He saw a car parked down the street that appeared to have some damage.

"Someone call the police," he yelled. He ran down to the car and when he arrived he stopped in terror.

There laid the body of his gay lover who was now his worst enemy. Brain matter was splattered on the passenger's window and blood was everywhere.

A few people stood in the parking lot and someone called the police. The detectives arrived on the scene along with the police and coroner.

Detective Black: Do you know who is responsible for this homicide?

Shawn: No. I heard gunshots as I was sitting in my car and ran down the street and found him like this.

Detective Sky: We would like you to come down to the station for some questions.

Shawn: Ok. Let me tell my wife first so she doesn't worry.

Connie was standing in the parking lot of the church with some of the church members.

Shawn: Donald was murdered. The police want to question me. I will go to the station with them. I will call you later for you to pick me up.

Connie: They don't think you did this do they?

Shawn: I don't know.

Even though Connie was disgusted with her husband, she still cared for him deep down. She didn't want to see him go to jail over something he didn't do. She managed to push her hurt to the side so she could focus on the chaos before her.

Shawn was interrogated for a couple of hours and the detectives realized that he was innocent so they let him go. Things were going to get much worse for Shawn. The last thing he needed was to be caught up in a murder investigation. "Who could've killed Donald? He was a very wicked man but he didn't deserve to be shot down in cold blood."

Connie picked her husband up from the station and there was little communication between them. She went to the bedroom and locked the door to rest while Shawn made his bed on the couch. He was exhausted. He had enough drama for one day. He just wanted to put everything far behind him and start over. "Was that bullet meant for me? Is my family safe?" There were so many questions swarming through Shawn's mind.

"They will find the murderer. The truth is going to be revealed. What's done in the dark is going to come to the light," he thought as he drifted off to sleep.

THREE HOURS EARLIER

The door to the farmhouse opened and Lisa walked inside her beautiful home. She was dressed in all black. She locked the door behind her. She puts the gun in a case in the back of her closet. "I couldn't take any more of your evil. You had to go," she thought.

Lisa was devastated about the fall of Shawn and the destruction of Connie and their marriage. She knew her friend was hurt and she had to intervene. "This will be my secret that I will take to the grave," she said out loud.

CHAPTER NINE

I LOST EVERYTHING

It was a beautiful hot sunny day outside but inside the Wayne household it was dreary. Shawn woke up on the couch and usually the day after a conference he would settle down for a while and focus on family. He and Connie would date by going to the movies or a restaurant then make love all over the house later that night.

However, his wife didn't want anything to do with him. Connie had practically locked herself in the bedroom. She wasn't her usual self. Shawn knew that he was the source of her pain. He hoped in his heart that she would forgive him one day. Normally Connie would prepare a huge breakfast but since his secret was exposed the pots and pans were unused. Connie was too distraught to eat. She really had no appetite.

Shawn laid on the couch and felt empty. He wished he hadn't sinned against God because he hurt a lot of people. "How could I be so selfish. I took the devil's bait," he thought. It seemed like an eternity passed by before Connie came out of the bedroom. She was thirsty and hadn't drank anything since yesterday. Shawn could hear her walking down the stairs and into the kitchen. He sat up on the couch. He wanted to love on his wife and make things right.

Connie walked into the kitchen and her hair was displaced. Her eye makeup was smeared from crying throughout the night. Her robe was hanging off her shoulders exposing her tank top beneath. The sound of her slippers skidded across the floor. She paused at the refrigerator and pulled out a bottle of cold water. She opened it and began to quench her thirst as the water guzzled down her throat. She let out a sigh, "Aah," because the drink was so refreshing.

At that moment Shawn walked into the kitchen and his wife looked at him. "I'm going to go say something to her. I'm not going to sit on the couch all day in silence." He was a little taken back by her appearance and his heart broke more when he saw how he tore down the woman he promised to love and to cherish for life. "I'm sorry babe," he said.

Connie: Look! I don't have anything to say to you!

She begins to walk away but Shawn grabs her by her arms and pulls her into his chest. Connie tried to break free but her husband's strength overpowered her.

Connie: Let me go please!

His touch on her skin repulsed her. It reminded her of all the hurt he caused her.

Shawn: Babe! I messed up! Please forgive me! I love you! I need you by my side!

Connie: Love? Love doesn't cheat! I gave you sex anytime you wanted! It wasn't good enough! You chose a man over me! Gross!

At that moment she managed to break free of his grip. She dashed up the stairs and slammed the bedroom behind her. Her response was like a dagger in Shawn's heart. Tears filled the corner of his eyes. He paused to regroup his feelings then dashed up the stairs. He approached the bedroom door and twisted the knob. It was locked. He began to bang on the door. Shawn and Connie began to converse. When she heard the banging on the door she sat on the edge of the bed. Tears ran down her face.

Shawn: Open the door! I'm still your husband!

Connie: Leave me alone! I have nothing to say to you!

Shawn: Look, babe! I'm not going anywhere. I made a mistake! It hurts me to see the pain that I caused!

Connie: You lied to me! You said it was a one-time thing in your office, but I found out that was a lie with the rest of the church when they saw another man sucking your penis!

Shawn: I'm sorry that I lied! I swear that it only happened twice. He tricked me and seduced me. I tried to end it but he went psycho.

Connie: How do you expect me to feel? I can't even look at you right now without seeing that video!

Shawn: I know, babe. I screwed up! I can't even look at myself!

Connie: You just expect me to forgive you just like that? I'm embarrassed! Now everything makes sense! People were looking at me the other day in the grocery store because they must have seen the video online. Everyone knew about your little love affair, and I was made a fool out of.

Shawn: I'm so sorry.

Connie: Do I need to get tested for HIV? You put my safety on the line. How can you say you love me?

He ignored his wife's question because he never thought about the possibility of giving sexually transmitted diseases to his wife when he was indulging in sin.

Shawn: Please tell me what I need to do to make things right.

Connie: I don't know if we will ever be right again. All I see is that video in my mind. I was willing to work it out and move past this, but you lied and made me look a fool! You hurt a lot of people. No wonder the parking lot was empty at the conference yesterday...because everyone all over the United States knows you are the pastor on the down-low that got caught. How awful!

He paused and thought about what his next response should be. "She is right, " he thought.

Shawn: I pray you will forgive me one day. I will never hurt you again. I promise.

Connie: To be honest. Your words don't mean anything to me. I want a divorce. I don't want to be married to a pastor on the down-low . How do I know that you will never cheat again? I can't live in paranoia. Now when I look at men, I start to wonder if you will sleep with them too.

Shawn: Don't say that. I will get help. I swear! I will get counseling. Whatever it takes.

Connie: I want you out! Get out! Find another place to live!

Shawn was taken back. He was devastated because Connie never spoke to him like this before. He knew that she was serious. He needed to clear his head.

He went back to the living room and picked up his phone. He had so many missed calls and notifications from social media. When he went on his social media app, his heart dropped because he saw that thousands of people had viewed the sex video. Shawn felt sick to his stomach as he saw the cruel names people called him. He was the subject of many jokes and hot topics. Suddenly the taste of vomit filled his mouth, and he ran to the bathroom, but unfortunately, his stomach was empty so he couldn't throw up. After a few dry heaves, he washed out his mouth with some water and left the house.

Shawn got in his car and headed to the church. He wanted to find a way to connect back to God. He knew that if He truly repented, then perhaps God could restore Him. When he pulled up to the church, some reporters we're outside. They surrounded his car. Shawn managed to maneuver through the crowd and into the church.

"Mr. Wayne, what are your remarks on the sex video? Did you kill Donald? Can you tell your side of the story?" the reporters yelled.

Shawn: No comment!

Shawn closed the doors in the reporters' faces. He went into his office and began to weep. He sees a photo of his wife and him on his desk and cries uncontrollably. His world was collapsing.

Suddenly his phone started to ring. He knew he had to answer it because it was the local church council. He knew they provided funding to his ministry and he was a part of the board.

Shawn: Hello.

Apostle Gray: Pastor Shawn. How are you?

Shawn: Not good.

Apostle Gray: I know you are probably in a low place and we are praying for you. I'm sorry to have to do this. The board has decided to halt funding to your ministry and we are sitting you down for three years before you can do any public ministry. Please clear out your office and turn in your keys. It's not personal. I hope you understand.

Shawn: Yes, I understand. Thank you.

Shawn hung up the phone. He put his head in his hands and took a deep breath. He began to pack up his belongings into a box that he found in the closet. Regret consumed him. "I will miss this place. It was my second home," he thought.

He held the box tightly in his arms. He walked towards the door and saw a bunch of reporters still outside the church. Seeing them brought him back to the reality of the consequences of his sins. "Father, if you can hear me please give me the strength to face this, " he prayed. He took a deep breath, opened the door, walked through the crowd, got in his car, and drove away.

When he got home, Connie had already packed all of his clothes and belongings. His stuff was sitting in suitcases in the living room. When he saw his things he felt rage and hurt. He rushed upstairs and started banging on the locked door.

Shawn: Connie! Have you gone mad? I pay bills in this house! I'm not going anywhere!

Connie: Go! Or I will call the police!

Shawn: Wow!

He knew that she meant those words so he turned around and grabbed his things. He put the suitcases in his car, drove downtown, and checked into a nice hotel room.

When he entered the room, he didn't bother to unpack. Shawn laid across the bed. He cut off his phone because there were so many notifications. The sight of them overwhelmed him.

"I just need rest and a plan to move forward." He thought about life as he drifted off into a deep sleep. The exhaustion and pain had finally caught up to him. Shawn would need every ounce of rest because doom was waiting around the corner to take him into a deeper pit.

CHAPTER TEN

DEATH IS WAITING

Six months went by, and Shawn was living on his own in an apartment in a gated community. Even though he wasn't preaching in circles with his denomination, he was still ministering. People heard of his ministry and still wanted the gifts on his life. They didn't care about his character and wanted him to come to their churches because he attracted crowds and knew how to raise large offerings. He would receive a huge honorarium from these meetings that sustained him financially. Since Shawn did not submit to his leaders and sit down for three years like he was told, he was excommunicated and marked as rebellious among the faith leaders in various organizations. "Well I have to support myself. I'm not sinning now. I will never sin against God again because I lost everything, " he thought.

Even though Shawn was ministering he still felt lost and far from God. He was dealing with a spirit of condemnation, shame, guilt, fear, and depression. He suffered from nightmares and sometimes he could see the scene where the blood of Donald was scattered everywhere. Sometimes he would cry because he was overwhelmed by the pressures of life. He yearned for the peace of God that he once felt daily. He desired to hear the voice of God again when he prayed. He felt like he was going through the motions yet he remained hopeful to get back in right standing with God.

He hadn't spoken to Connie in months, and he missed her. He tried calling her several times over the months, but she never answers. He asked some people about her and they told him that she seems to be really happy and her candle business was doing well. Connie had filed for divorce and served Shawn with paperwork. There was a knock on his apartment door.

Man: Are you Shawn Wayne?

Shawn: Yes.

Man: You have been served.

The man handed him a document and walked off. When he opened it, his heart started to bleed as he saw the words "MOTION OF DISSOLUTION OF MARRIAGE."

"Wow. I guess this is it. Connie hates me and never wants to see me again," he thought.

After he was served, he stopped trying to contact her. He decided to move on as best he could until the court date, which was a few months ahead. He knew he had to try to rebuild his reputation, so he landed a few interviews on the radio to explain his side of the story. His explanation helped generate buzz around him and support, but it was not to the magnitude of how it was before he fell. People never forgot about his sexual immorality because ever so often someone would bring it back up again and call him names. Shawn was the hot topic in the Christian community for months.

One day after Shawn finished preaching at a conference, his throat started to hurt. He didn't think it was unusual because he lost his voice before when he preached too hard. So when he got home, he drank some hot tea. He relaxed, watched a few videos of his favorite drama series, and went to bed.

The next day, he noticed that his lymph nodes in his throat were swollen, and he had a fever. It was hard for him to swallow. He took some Tylenol to regulate his temperature and just rested his body. He dozed off for an hour and when he woke up, he realized that he hadn't eaten yet, so he went into the kitchen to eat some lunch. He started to feel so weak, and his stomach didn't feel the best, but he pressed through it and made himself a turkey and cheese sandwich. He figured a sandwich was a quick fix and not too heavy on an upset stomach. He was able to digest the food properly and put a cold rag on his forehead to cool off. "This must be backlash from the message I gave yesterday, " he thought.

Weeks went by and he didn't feel any better but he managed to function. "Maybe I'm over exerting myself, " he thought. He never said no to engagements because he needed to make money. He figured it was just spiritual warfare and he would believe God for healing. However Shawn failed to realize that the spirit of the Lord left his life months ago. Every time he ministered it was from his gifts; yet, the calling and gifts of God are irrevocable.

One night during a conference, Shawn was the guest speaker. He preached an encouraging word about new beginnings. People were really blessed by the message and they started to praise God. While Shawn was speaking, he paused and gripped the side of the podium. He started to feel extremely weak because he used every ounce of energy to pour out to the crowd. His legs felt like rubber and gave out from beneath him. He collapsed on the floor and people began to gasp. Some people rushed around him, laid hands on him, prayed for him, and helped him sit up. One of the ushers gave him water to drink and someone called the ambulance.

Shawn couldn't believe what was happening. He felt as if his life was slipping away. Some men helped Shawn off the floor and sat him up in a chair. When the paramedics came, they took his vital signs and they discovered that he was feverish. They administered medication and oxygen because his breathing was labored. Shawn felt drained and blacked out in the back of the ambulance. When he arrived at the hospital, they drew blood and ran tests. A nurse asked him if he had a last will and testament. He replied no because he hadn't thought that far ahead and he figured that he was too young to die. She asked if he had an emergency contact and he realized that he had no one to be by his side. So he just put down Connie's name since she was still his wife.

A few hours after being admitted to the hospital a doctor came into the room and told him that he was terminally ill and he had cancer that had metastasized to his lungs and he had an infection in his blood. The doctor told him that he was dying and that death was imminent. "What?" he said. "How?" he asked. "I was in total health six months ago."

The doctor explained that certain factors such as foods, lifestyle, genes and environmental exposures like chemicals or toxins could accelerate abnormal cell growth. Shawn didn't understand and panic set in. The doctor ordered him some medication to help him to relax and be comfortable. A respiratory therapist came and gave him a breathing treatment to treat the wheezing in his airways.

After his respiration normalized and he settled into his room he reflected on everything. "My sins opened the door for the enemy to bring sickness upon me. The devil's job is to kill, steal, and destroy. The devil has really done all those things to me. Here I am in this hospital, and I'm going to die alone. Holding on to secrets, hurt, bitterness, self-rejection, condemnation, and hatred allowed the spirit of cancer and death to enter my soul. I can't believe the things that I used to preach against and tell people not to do that I ended up committing the same offense."

At that moment, Shawn did something that he struggled to do for months. As he prayed tears streamed down his face.

"Lord, I come before you humbly. I know I haven't prayed in a while. I felt so far from you and to be honest, I haven't even forgiven myself for the horrible things I've done. I was scared to come to you and I avoid facing you. Please forgive me. I'm sorry for hurting the people who loved me. I'm sorry for bringing you shame. I repent of my sins. I'm sorry for lying, committing adultery, hurting you and others, being a hypocrite, and not being a good steward over the gifts you gave me. Please forgive me for being disobedient to you and leaders and for doing things in my own strength and not yours. I know now that homosexuality wrong and I can't inherit the kingdom of God living that lifestyle. Don't let me die Lord. Please heal me."

After he prayed, he felt a release because this was the first time in months that he gave God everything in his heart.

TWO WEEKS LATER

Shawn and Chaplain George talked for a while.

Chaplain Sam: Wow. That is some story. Don't feel bad. We all make mistakes. God is merciful and He loves you so much. You will get past this because the Bible promises us victory. How do you feel now that you have gotten everything off your chest?

Shawn: I feel better and much lighter.

Chaplain Sam: Great. Let's pray before I go. I'll come back tomorrow to check on you.

Shawn: Ok.

Little did both men know that tomorrow would never come for Shawn.

Chaplain Sam: Dear Heavenly Father, bless Shawn and heal him now. Give him peace, comfort, and strength to get through this trying time. Forgive him of his transgressions and bless him with a fresh start. Allow him to feel close to you yet again. Lord let your will be done. Amen.

Shawn: Amen.

The two men shook hands and Chaplain George left out of the room. Shawn felt peace again for the first time in months. "Yes! The Lord heard our prayers!" he thought. He smiled and he adjusted the covers. He closed his eyes and slipped into eternity.

ABOUT THE AUTHOR

Kimberly Moses started off her ministry as Kimberly Hargraves. She is highly sought after as a prophetic voice, intercessor and prolific author. There is no doubt that she has a global mandate on her life to serve the nations of the world by spreading the Gospel of Jesus Christ. She has a quickly expanding worldwide healing and deliverance ministry. Kimberly Moses wears many hats to fulfill the call God has placed on her life as an entrepreneur over several businesses including her own personal brand Rejoice Essentials which promotes the Gospel of Jesus Christ.

She also serves as a life coach and mentor to many women. She is also the loving mother of two wonderful children. She is married to Tron. Kimberly has dedicated her life to the work of ministry and to serve others under the call God has placed over her life. Kimberly currently resides in South Carolina.

She is a very anointed woman of God who signs, miracles and wonders follow. The miraculous and incessant testimonies attributed to her ministry are incalculable, with many reporting physical and mental healing, financial breakthroughs, debt cancellations and other favorable outcomes. She is known across the globe as a servant who truly labors on behalf of God's people through intercession.

She is the author of The Following:

"Overcoming Difficult Life Experiences with Scriptures and Prayers"
"Overcoming Emotions with Prayers"
"Daily Prayers That Bring Changes"
"In Right Standing,"
"Obedience Is Key,"
"Prayers That Break The Yoke Of The Enemy: A Book Of Declarations,"
"Prayers That Demolish Demonic Strongholds: A Book Of Declarations,"
"Work Smarter. Not Harder. A Book Of Declarations For The Workforce,"
"Set The Captives Free: A Book Of Deliverance."
"Pray More Challenge"
"Walk By Faith: A Daily Devotional"
"Empowering The New Me: Fifty Tips To Becoming A Godly Woman"
"School of the Prophets: A Curriculum For Success"
"8 Keys To Accessing The Supernatural"
"Conquering The Mind: A Daily Devotional"
"Enhancing The Prophetic In You"
"The ABCs of The Prophetic: Prophetic Characteristics"

"Wisdom Is The Principal Thing: A Daily Devotional"
"It Cost Me Everything"
"The Making Of A Prophet: Women Walking in Prophetic Destiny"
"The Art of Meditation: A Daily Devotional"
"Warfare Strategies: Biblical Weapons"
"Becoming A Better You"
"I Almost Died"

You can find more about Kimberly at
www.kimberlyhargraves.com

For Rejoice Essential Magazine
www.rejoiceessential.com

For Beauty Products
www.rejoicingbeauty.com

Please write a review for my books on Amazon.com

Support this ministry:
Cashapp: $ProphetessKim
Paypal.me/remag

COMING SOON

PART 2

WHAT THE THERAPIST DIDN'T WANT YOU TO KNOW

Sarah was a beautiful Occupational Therapist who is married to Walter. However, Sarah has a terrible secret that if exposed, she will lose everything. Find out how the story goes.

www.ingramcontent.com/pod-product-compliance
Lightning Source LLC
Chambersburg PA
CBHW072027110526
44592CB00012B/1417